INSIDE THE
Korean House

Architecture and Design
In the Contemporary Hanok

NANI PARK and ROBERT J. FOUSER
Photography by JONGKEUN LEE

TUTTLE Publishing
Tokyo │ Rutland, Vermont │ Singapore

CONTENTS

Preface

Gangnam Style, K-Pop, *kimchee*, *bulgogi*, "Winter Sonata" and "Daejanggum"—these are the words that most commonly come to mind when foreigners think of Korea. While these cultural icons have contributed immensely to the popularity of Korean music, cuisine and television viewing at home and abroad, they are only a small part of Korean history, tradition and culture. My aim in this book is to expand readers' awareness of Korea by adding another word, one that is an integral part of Korean architectural history and, with it, culture. The word is *hanok* and it refers to the traditional wooden house structure that originated in the Joseon Dynasty in the late fourteenth century.

As a one and a half generation Korean-American, returning to live in Korea was not an easy adjustment for me. During my first two years in Korea, I developed a love–hate relationship with my old–new home. My return was a constant process of learning to assimilate into a culture that I had left behind when I was a mere eight years old. Being bilingual helped tremendously with the transition, but the Korea I remembered was old-fashioned, distant and quaint compared to the bustling concrete jungle that now surrounded me. My fondest memory of my childhood was of running through our neighborhood, a maze of narrow winding paths that separated *hanok*, and the seemingly endless waves of tiled roofs. Reminiscing on my childhood home in my very own *hanok* is where I got the idea for this book.

I believe anything old is new again and people yearn to return to the basics. Many Koreans today are growing up walled off, surrounded by concrete partitions separating them from the world outside. They long for an environmentally friendly architectural space of their own. One of the *hanok* featured in this book is owned by a popular interior designer who is involved in the social media community of Korea. Whenever he tweets or posts photos of his *hanok*, his young followers comment how envious they are and how they would love a *hanok* of their own. Living in a *hanok* is now considered trendy!

A few years ago, when visiting a friend's newly built *hanok*, I was amazed by the interior. Whereas the exterior remained traditional, the inside of her home was completely modern. It was the opposite of what I remembered about early *hanok*. I began to search for books on these distinctive traditional Korean homes to satisfy my curiosity, but it was quickly apparent that very little had been published in English (or Korean) about them. Detailed descriptions are essential in understanding the history and the reasoning behind structures like *hanok*. I felt that the integral aspects of *hanok*—their beauty, harmony and simplicity—could best be demonstrated through a photographic book with accompanying text. I wanted readers to be able to imagine themselves in one of these honorable and elegant houses.

In order to turn my dream into reality, I had to find twelve representative *hanok* that showed style and taste. The process of locating, selecting and receiving permission to enter and publicize these homes was the most difficult challenge in producing the book. Not only did I have to search hard for these homes, I had to make sure they represented the complete range of *hanok*, from old to new, and be of sufficient size and within the city limits. I wanted to show how the *hanok* has fared over the years and how it has changed to suit modern needs while remaining historically appealing. Once I was able to identify my ideal group of *hanok*, I next had to seek permission from the owners to write about and photograph their homes. I shall be forever grateful to these people for opening up their private living spaces to my team, thereby giving readers, far and wide, a rare glimpse into the Korean *hanok* experience.

One of the owners whose home is featured in the book told me that building a *hanok* was like a circus. Both require many "performers," each dependent on the collaboration and cooperation of the others for success. A *hanok*'s beauty and durability depends on the architect who has to understand the materials and the steps in the construction processes; the stonemason who chisels rocks and lays the foundation; the carpenter who erects wooden support beams and other members without using a single nail; the roof tiler who achieves both function and beauty with his care; the paper expert who covers wood-framed windows and doors and walls. Every part of the process is done by specialists using only the finest natural materials—earth, stone, wood and paper—in an integrated sequence. According to Korean philosophy, humans are born into the world with no possessions and leave without a trace. *Hanok* are similar; all that remains is the foundation. The philosophy of life that Koreans live by is still apparent in a *hanok*, whether modern or traditional in style, and the concept of harmony with nature is constant.

It is now over fifteen years since I returned to Korea and I can say unreservedly that my relationship with my homeland is one of love above anything else because of my deeper appreciation of all that it has to offer. My hope is that readers will appreciate and understand the Korean *hanok* as a piece of architectural history, as a way of preserving Korean culture and as a thing of beauty.

—Nani Park

Introduction

A walk through Seoul brings to mind *bibimbap*, the colorful mixed rice and vegetable dish that has come to represent Korean food in the minds of many. Like *bibimbap*, Seoul has distinct forms of architecture that mix to create the electric unified whole that defies easy description. To many, this "mixed Seoul" appears light gray at first glance, but it soon turns that image on its head as bold colors and unique designs catch the eye upon closer examination.

The "mixed Seoul" of today, of course, is a new city, a product of nearly a half century of rapid economic growth since industrialization began in the early 1960s. Before the boom, Seoul looked more uniform as traditional architectural ideas and practices created a more orderly cityscape. Seoul was founded in 1394 as the capital of the Joseon Dynasty that ruled Korea until 1910. From its founding to the end of the nineteenth century, Seoul was an ocean of tile and thatched roofs with official buildings popping up like islands. All buildings in Seoul were built of wood and used natural materials, such as stone and paper. Like many Asian cities, a wall surrounded the city and only residents were allowed on the inside after dark. Four large gates and four smaller gates in the wall controlled the flow of people and goods into the city.

Toward the end of the nineteenth century, foreign powers, both Western and Asian, began to fight for hegemony over Korea. Japan eventually won the day and subjected Korea to colonial rule from 1910 to 1945. During the late nineteenth century, foreign missionaries, diplomats and traders brought Western architectural styles to Korea and brick churches and multi-floor box-like buildings began to pierce the traditional cityscape. The streetscape changed, too, as roads were widened and paved to make way for streetcars.

The Japanese colonial period brought rapid change to Seoul as Japan sought to integrate Korea deeply into the Japanese economy. As part of that effort, Japan turned Seoul, which it had renamed as Keijo, into a regional administrative city that was subservient to central power in Tokyo. Japan built imposing public buildings, some of which remain today, to house modern Japanese institutions: schools, hospitals, post offices and police stations. Many of these buildings were built on sites that once held detached palaces and other official buildings. Architecture related to Korean cultural heritage, meanwhile, was recast to represent Korean culture as "local culture" within greater Japan. Many of the buildings in Gyeongbokgung Palace, for example, were demolished (most of the wood, stones and roof tiles were reused) and the headquarters of the colonial government was built on the grounds in 1926, leaving the remaining palace buildings as touches of local color for tourists.

The later years of Japanese colonial rule brought industrialization and a surge in the population of Seoul. Japan's seizure of Manchuria in 1931 and invasion of China proper in 1937 turned Korea into an important base for military operations. Seoul became a magnate for people from other regions of Korea and from Japan proper. The city expanded beyond the wall, and parts of which were destroyed to make way for roads and buildings. The housing shortage of the 1920s became acute in the 1930s, forcing the colonial government to encourage the construction of new housing. Large plots of "developable land" inside the wall were divided into small plots to allow for greater density and new areas of tract housing outside the wall were developed.

The housing boom in the 1930s stimulated the development of new forms of residential architecture. One of the most experimental forms was the "city *hanok*" that emerged in the late 1920s and 1930s. The word *hanok* is used to refer to traditional Korean houses of various sizes. *Han* means "Korea" and *ok* means "house." As a genre of residential architecture, the *hanok* is most noted for its use of heated floors, known as *ondol*, which originated thousands of years ago in the Korean Peninsula for heating in the cold winter. The *ondol* heating system used timber to heat a fire in a stove next to the house. Heat from the fire spread under the floor, heating the stones in the process. Smoke escaped through a chimney, and the stones of the floor were covered with oiled paper to prevent any smoke from coming into the room. The same fire was also used for cooking. Because timber was limited, heated rooms were small and had small windows. *Hanok* also had unheated rooms with wood floors. These rooms were larger, had more windows and were used mainly in the warmer seasons.

Over thousands of years, the *hanok* has adapted well to the Korean climate and the practical needs of residents. The mixture of heated and unheated rooms saves energy and helps make the house comfortable throughout the year. Below the tiles on the roof is a layer of dirt that helps insulate the house in the winter and cool it in the summer. The eaves of the roof are short enough to allow sunlight to enter the house in the winter but long enough to keep it away during the summer. The eaves also help keep rain from hitting the house, which protects the wood. The posts sit on stone bases, which prevent them from rotting. The paper windows breathe and allow light into the house but keep out wind and help retain heat in the winter.

Like other types of vernacular architecture, *hanok* were built by master carpenters who designed the house on site, often as it was being built. The process of building a *hanok* starts with preparing the stone bases and the foundation for the heated floor. The frame of wooden posts and beams goes up next, followed by the roof. After the frame and roof are up, the walls of clay and rice straw are built and the floors are put in. The final stage of construction consists of attaching the windows and papering the heated floors, walls and windows. Traditionally, *hanok* were built of the following four elements: wood, stone, clay (including roof tiles) and paper. A small amount of iron was used for hinges and locks.

PREVIOUS SPREAD Colorful contemporary art of a woman in traditional Korean dress creates an attractive contrast between new and old in a room with a traditional paper-covered floor.

RIGHT AND PAGE 13 Spending time in a *hanok* allows you to observe its many practical and artistic details. Designs at the end of roof tiles, for example, use a wide range of playful motifs based on symbolically important flowers, mythological creatures and Chinese characters.

The size and structure of a *hanok* varied with social class. Aristocrats lived in estates that consisted of several elegant structures with tile roofs. The men's quarters, or *sarangchae*, was where the senior man of the house lived, studied and entertained guests. It combined elegance with minimalist aesthetics. The women's quarters, or *anchae*, was larger and was where women lived and raised children. The kitchen was attached to this part of the house. The two parts of the house were close to each other but were separated by a wall. Estates also had a number of servants who lived in the servants' quarters, or *hengnangchae*, located near to the other two buildings. Behind the kitchen was an area for storing *kimchi* and other condiments. Many estates also had a small ancestral shrine, or *sadang*, that was used in annual ceremonies in honor of ancestors. Peasant houses, by contrast, were usually a simple structure with a few rooms and a thatched roof. In Seoul and several other provincial centers, lower-ranking bureaucrats and merchants lived in smaller houses with tile roofs.

Built on small lots that were divided from larger lots, city *hanok* applied traditional *hanok* building principles to the new urban environment of limited space. Built of wood, city *hanok* had curving tile roofs typical of the larger houses in Seoul up to the end of the nineteenth century. They used many of the same materials, for example stone for heated floors and paper to cover the floors and walls. The kitchen was reduced in size but was still lower than the rest of the house so that heat from cooking fires could flow under the floor of neighboring rooms in winter. Though criticized for crowding too many people into a small space, the city *hanok* proved popular and spread quickly in old areas of the city inside the wall and to expanding areas outside the wall.

As products of the industrial age, city *hanok* included innovations that made use of new materials pouring out of local factories. Bricks replaced stones for exterior walls and glass replaced paper in the windows. Large glass windows facing the courtyard often had a set of paper-covered windows on the inside that helped to keep out drafts in the cold Seoul winters. The interior courtyard, or *madang*, was often paved in concrete with tile covering the border areas. The small lots required a number of design changes. Limited space, for example, made it difficult to dedicate space for long eaves so these were shortened and gutters installed to catch rainwater. The houses, each with an interior courtyard, came in standard shapes similar to letters of the Korean *hangeul* writing system. Large houses were shaped like the letter *mieum* (ㅁ), mid-sized houses like the letter *digeut* (ㄷ) and small houses like the letter *giyeok* (ㄱ). Odd-shaped lots made for some exceptions but most conformed to one of these patterns.

The most famous place for city *hanok* in Seoul is the Bukchon neighborhood that sits between Gyeongbokgung Palace and Changdeokgung Palace. The houses in Gahoe-dong, the most photographed part of the neighborhood, were built in the mid-1930s by Segwon Jeong (1888–1965), a house builder who is credited with developing the city *hanok* style. Jeong was part of the cultural nationalist movement that began in the 1920s. Demonstrations advocating Korean independence spread around the nation on March 1, 1919. The Japanese put down the demonstrations but adopted a more lenient form of rule. Newspapers in Korean appeared and Korean cultural activity increased. The cultural nationalists were interested in promoting Korean

FOLLOWING SPREAD Dusk in mid-summer in Seoul brings a breeze into the courtyard and through the house. As in a traditional *hanok*, the courtyard here functions as an extension of the living space but with a modern twist: a glass roof between the two wings of the house allows the courtyard-cum-patio to be used on rainy days.

cultural activity in order to preserve Korean identity amid the weight of Japanese rule. The wealthy Jeong knew many of the movement's leaders and contributed financially to their cause.

Like many preservation activists today, Jeong feared that development would destroy the Korean character of the city. Large lots that once held aristocratic estates in Bukchon were in danger because owners who had fallen on hard times after the collapse of the Joseon Dynasty in 1910 were being forced to sell their property to survive. Jeong wanted to prevent the Japanese from moving in, so he bought much of Gahoe-dong with the intention of developing it in Korean style.

Segwon Jeong's Korean style first developed in Ikseon-dong, an area south of Bukchon that has become a "*hanok* island" in the center of Seoul. In 1930, Jeong bought a large plot of empty land where a small detached royal palace once stood. He divided the land into smaller lots and put alleys in between them for access. Lots in different alleys varied in size so that houses of different sizes could be built. In this new space, he first tested the construction of city *hanok* on a large scale. The houses, of varying shapes and sizes, were built en masse and then sold after construction ended. The roots of the city *hanok* remain clearly on display in Ikseon-dong today: rows of houses with brick walls, short eaves, glass windows and brick and tile walls. Front doors lead into small courtyards that provide access to all the rooms. In Ikseon-dong, Jeong achieved his goal of a developing a "Korean-style house for Koreans" and later applied the lessons learned to Gahoe-dong, his magnum opus.

By the late 1930s, the Japanese war effort brought residential construction to a halt. In 1942, the thirty-three core members of the Korean Language Society were sent to jail as "subversives" and Jeong's assets were confiscated because of his support for the group. The dark years of World War II were followed by political turmoil after liberation in August of 1945. Competition between the United States and the Soviet Union exacerbated the turmoil and led to the creation of two states in 1948. In 1950, North Korea invaded South Korea, leading to a bitter war that ended with a ceasefire in 1953. The war left both Koreas in ruins.

Recovery from the war was slow in South Korea, but it moved forward. Damage to Bukchon was minimal because the city changed hands quickly as the front line moved south and then north. As Korea recovered from the war, construction of city *hanok* resumed, though not on the mass scale of the 1930s, and continued until the mid-1960s.

The Korean economy took off in the mid-1960s, which caused the population of Seoul and other major cities to surge as young people poured into the cities to fill jobs in booming factories. To deal with the housing shortage, the government focused its efforts on building apartment complexes. The economic boom and incumbent social change caused Koreans to turn away from their cultural heritage and to embrace, in particular, Western and American lifestyles. The combination of government policy and social change caused the city *hanok* to fall out of favor, causing carpenters, roofers and stone cutters to look for work in other fields. By the 1990s, only a handful of skilled *hanok* craftsmen remained and most worked on restoring and maintaining cultural relics.

Perhaps because of its location between the two most important royal palaces, Bukchon always had a special place in the hearts and minds of Korean architects and cultural activists. Famous architect Swoogeun Kim (1931–86), for example, grew up in Bukchon, as did many other luminary cultural figures of the twentieth century. From its beginning in the mid-1930s to the early 1970s, Bukchon was home to educated and well-off Koreans. After prestigious high schools in Bukchon moved to newly developed areas south of the Hangang River in the mid-1970s, property values began to decline as wealthy Koreans moved out. By the late 1970s, architects and others began to worry about the future of Bukchon and encouraged the city government to take a more active role in preservation. In 1984, the government responded by creating the Gahoe-dong Hanok Preservation District. The move prevented any construction that altered the appearance of the *hanok* but this frustrated residents who wanted to update their house to changing lifestyles.

As Seoul boomed in the last third of the twentieth century, the city *hanok* was on the verge of extinction. The situation greatly worsened in the early 1990s after changes in building laws allowed the construction of multi-floor, multi-family dwellings on the small lots of land where *hanok* once stood. In the span of a few years, *hanok* and other low-rise houses were destroyed at a torrid pace and replaced by three- and four-story multi-family dwellings. The destruction even spread to Bukchon, particularly after restrictions on new construction in the preservation district were lifted. Construction companies eager to build apartment complexes approached residents in areas with a high concentration of *hanok* and encouraged them to participate in redevelopment, which meant demolishing the entire neighborhood and building an apartment complex. As apartment prices soared, the lure of a making a profit by leaving an aging, inconvenient house was too strong to ignore and many residents become supporters of redevelopment.

After the massive wave of *hanok* destruction in the early 1990s, preservationists and the city government became alarmed and began work on plans to protect what was left of Bukchon. Recognizing that the rigid restrictions of the 1980s left owners unhappy and houses in bad condition, the city decided to adopt a system of incentives to help owners renovate their houses. The system

PREVIOUS SPREAD Paper is an important material in *hanok*. Windows, which also serve as doors, are covered with paper that is replaced every couple of years. This room has screens—a modern convenience—that run behind the papered windows and the exterior windows.

LEFT Many older large *hanok* dating from the early twentieth century have Western-style rooms, mostly for entertaining foreign guests, but with traditional Korean details.

offered an outright cash grant combined with a no-interest loan to *hanok* owners who renovated their houses according to architecture and design guidelines. As word of the coming change spread, aficionados of traditional Korean culture began to buy *hanok* in Bukchon with the aim of renovating them. By the early 2000s, the economy had recovered from the 1997 economic crisis and renovations to *hanok* in Bukchon began in earnest and continue, albeit at a slower pace, today.

The first wave of renovations caused controversy because it changed the appearance of the houses considerably. Preservationists were alarmed at the extent of the changes and began to complain that the scale of the renovations went beyond what was necessary and, in some cases, equaled new construction. Architects and builders, meanwhile, argued that the houses needed a full-scale gut renovation or, in some cases, complete reconstruction so that they could be updated to contemporary needs. The city's design guidelines complicated the matter because they required owners to abandon the aesthetics of the city *hanok* in favor of traditional Joseon-period aesthetics of the eighteenth and nineteenth centuries. Sliding glass windows were replaced by outward-opening windows with a dense lattice typical of traditional Korean design. Traditional Korean paper was pasted onto glass panes to make the windows look traditional. This created a neo-traditional or "neo-Joseon" style that evoked images of rural gentry, or *yangban*, living in country estates.

The pace of renovation began to slow in 2010 as the city turned its attention to Seochon, the neighborhood on the opposite side of Gyeongbokgung Palace. The area has a number of *hanok* and was threatened by redevelopment until 2008. To counter the pressure for redevelopment, the city applied the same system of incentives for renovation to Seochon. As the city's interest shifted to Seochon, controversies in Bukchon began moving toward a tentative conclusion. Growing interest in *hanok* contributed to a greater appreciation of city *hanok* and the history behind them. Examples of innovative, often bold, designs have shown that *hanok* can be updated to contemporary needs and tastes. The tentative conclusion coming from Bukchon thus suggests the emergence of a new genre of *hanok* that incorporate the aesthetics of city *hanok* from the 1930s and the neo-traditional style from the early 2000s: the "mixed *hanok*." This new genre allows for experimentation and, perhaps more importantly, the expression of the owner's personality. Like the city of Seoul itself, they appear similar from afar but sparkle with the color of individuality up close.

As Korea has matured in the early years of this century, *hanok* have become popular again. Busy, overworked baby boomers, many of whom were raised in a *hanok*, have rediscovered it as an environmentally friendly sanctuary that helps their well-being. Younger people, meanwhile, have discovered *hanok* for the first time and have taken to it as a way to escape the boredom of sterile apartment complexes. The houses in this book offer a look at a variety of "mixed *hanok*," some new and some old, that tell the story of how this unique Korean tradition has overcome the challenges of modernity to become the most innovative and beloved type of housing in Korea today.

—**Robert J. Fouser**

RIGHT *Hanok* interiors reflect the personality of the owner through a mixture of art and furniture. Exteriors tend to be more uniform, with variation found in how the building interacts with the surrounding natural environment.

Oidong Pyulchang

House in Oi-dong

우이동 별장

Moved from the center of Seoul in the 1950s, this is a rare example of a late nineteenth-century *hanok* estate house. Being the grandest structure in the estate, the house was located at the center of the property, which included several outer buildings. Typical of Korean *hanok* estates during the 1930s to mid-1950s, it was enclosed by a wall pierced by several gates for access.

In the mid-1950s there was intense pressure on owners to dismantle large estates and convert them into smaller lots to accommodate city *hanok*. The owners of this house were passionate about preserving Korean traditions after half a century of Japanese colonial rule and the rapid changes they witnessed after the Korean War (1950–3). Rather than destroy the house, they decided to move it to a secluded area on what was then the outskirts of Seoul. The move allowed them to reconstruct the original estate complex on the new property. The owners were pioneers for their time and the house continues to reflect the love and attention they lavished on it.

Inside the house, the most striking feature is the size of the main living room compared to a city *hanok*. The width of the room required long and sturdy crossbeams to support the high open ceiling with its exposed rafters. The height of the ceiling gives the room a sense of grandeur. Behind the main room is a Western-style dining room, once the location of the courtyard between the two wings of the house, which was added to the house for a more functional flow between the living room and kitchen.

The current owner of the *hanok* is a Swedish woman whose husband and his family owned the home. She came to Korea in the early 1960s after marrying, and raised two generations in the home. Every room contains examples of both heritages, Korean and Swedish. There is a wonderful mixture of traditional Korean art and furniture and family heirlooms from Sweden, including the chandelier that once belonged to her family in Sweden, which hangs prominently in the dining room. The owner proudly carries on the family tradition of caring for the house and, by extension, preserving Korean culture.

PREVIOUS SPREAD Sliding paper-covered doors frame the focal point of the Korean-style living room: a magnificent folding screen. The paintings on each panel include images of books, reflecting the historic reverence for learning in Korea. The room's raised floor, heated by the *ondol* system of hot water pipes under the floor, has been covered with Korean paper and varnished, making it waterproof and comfortable to walk and sit on.

RIGHT The formal dining room was built in what was once a courtyard and has a skylight that lets light in. The visual highlight of the room is the chandelier that once belonged to the owner's family in Sweden.

OPPOSITE The upholstered furniture in the Western-style living room complements the sturdy traditional beam-and-rafter structure supporting the heavy tile roof. The height of the roof, softened by hanging paper light shades, allows plenty of light into the room.

ABOVE, LEFT AND RIGHT A free-standing folding screen, chests both low and high decorated with beautiful brass fittings, and vivid silk floor cushions figure prominently in the traditional Korean living room that leads off the Western-style living room. The furnishings complement the glistening varnished paper on the raised floor, which is heated in winter by under-floor hot water pipes. The paper-covered sliding doors behind the bed beyond open to storage space and stairs that lead to a large attic.

ABOVE The dining room, like the living room, displays Korean antiques and objects that harmonize with the Western-style table setting.

OPPOSITE The living areas are decorated with an intriguing mix of Korean and Western antiques and ornamental objects that have been in the family for decades, many displayed for best effect against a background of paper-covered sliding doors.

ABOVE AND OPPOSITE The grounds surrounding the house offer ample space for displaying rustic antique Korean stone sculptures, such as a guardian figure from a tomb (above left) and a pagoda on a pedestal from a Buddhist temple (above right and opposite). The elegant lines of the sloping tiled roof, formed of adjacent layers of concave and convex tiles terminating in ornamental circular end tiles, are visible through the trees. An auspicious sign is placed above the entrance doors.

Yun Posun Residence

Residence of Yun Posun,
Second President of Korea

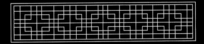

윤보선 고택

This house is undoubtedly the most famous *hanok* in Seoul. Occupying a large property on a picturesque street in Anguk-dong, the entrance to Bukchon, it is the last remaining example of a nineteenth-century *hanok* estate occupied by the same family for five generations. The house is located on Yun Posun Gil (street), named after its most famous resident, former President Yun Posun (1897–1990), the second president of the Republic of Korea (1960–2). President Yun remained active in politics long after his term finished and the house was an important meeting place for politicians. Today, the house, located on what was once the courtyard between the two wings of the house, is occupied by his son. Known simply as "President Yun Posun's house," it remains much loved by those who respect Yun Posun's efforts to help Korea become a thriving democracy.

Built around 1870, the estate consists of the main house where the family lives and several subsidiary houses and buildings. President Yun was educated at the University of Edinburgh and, after returning to Korea, decided to integrate Korean and Western culture. The creative blending of the two cultures is most evident and creative in the formal Western-style dining room, which former President Yun built for the comfort of foreign dignitaries. The dining room table, for example, is enhanced with inlaid mother-of-pearl Korean motifs and its edge has an upward-curving lip typical of traditional Korean tables. He also had dinnerware made that was suitable for both Western and Korean dining.

A high wall surrounds the entire estate and smaller walls border each of the other houses. This reflects the Korean tradition of dividing the estate into spaces for men, women and children, and servants. The family currently lives in the section of the house that was reserved for women and children. Over the years, the house has been renovated to meet the needs and conveniences of contemporary family living. The internal layout of the house, however, has remained the same, with each room retaining its original size and shape. Although maintenance and updating of the estate are ongoing, the original details are still evident, such as the location of the brick paths that were designed for viewing the houses from different angles to appreciate the gentle curve of the roofs. The house has been designated an Historical Site by the Korean Government and is often used to host events for worthy causes and for entertaining foreign dignitaries.

PREVIOUS SPREAD The furnishings in this living room, including the chairs arrayed around the walls, express both the formality and taste of Yun Posun. Adaptation to the climate, especially the summer heat, is also apparent in the rich paneling and the high ceiling with its exposed rafters and decorative wooden brackets.

RIGHT At first glance, the formal dining room looks Western, with its chandelier, fireplace and dining furniture, but Korean details are visible in the inlay on the table and the curved legs of the table and chairs. The diagonal lattice in the doors is especially ornate. Having a lattice on both sides of the doors (here the inner one is painted green), is relatively rare and the sign of a carefully made *hanok*.

LEFT President Yun frequently entertained here and had the yellow dinnerware specially made so that it would be suitable for both Korean and Western cuisine. An attractive feature in the room is the octagonal latticed ventilation windows on either side of the latticed doors.

RIGHT The fireplace in the formal dining room is flanked by ornate Korean chests, comfortable custom-made armchairs and bold ceramic jars. The dark hue of the wooden floor and furniture is offset by the pale yellow Korean silk papered walls and the red lacquered folding table and side tables.

38

ABOVE Metal pulls attached to the leaves of the windows on the terrace are molded in the shape of a lion's head. They were designed by President Yun, who received his Master's degree in archaeology from the University of Edinburgh. He drew on his experience in Scotland to create the hybrid Korean–Western style that makes this house unique.

RIGHT One of the most important aspects of a *hanok* is balance and symmetry. The long, narrow terrace in front of the windows is found only in large houses. It provides a layer of privacy when the windows are open in the warmer months. The large blossoming tree in front, a species of the rose family (*Rosa rugosa*), softens the symmetry and linearity of the house.

OPPOSITE, CLOCKWISE FROM TOP LEFT The house is full of wonderful detail, such as the beautifully curving tiled roof of the guest house that allows water to drain off, an old brass ashtray on a highly polished table, the imposing roofed pedestrian gate to the guest house, and the lacquered dining table with traditional upward-curling lip.

ABOVE A rare red lacquer table with woven rattan inset provides a vivid contrast to the dark wood of President Yun's customized hybrid Korean–Western armchair.

LEFT With its dark wood and Korean antiques, this sitting room in the main house evokes the rusticity of the early twentieth-century Arts and Crafts movement. Wooden screens with vertical and horizontal rodding slide in front of glass panes to modulate the amount of natural light in the room. The upholstered chairs by Korean designer Youngbaek Min blend beautifully with the antique chest in the center of the room, once used for holding money and valuables. The finely woven mat on the floor is for summer use and is replaced with a carpet in winter.

ABOVE Surrounded by gardens, the guest house also serves as a place for intimate gatherings. President Yun liked to entertain here during the summer months. The lines of the hip-and-gable roof, its wooden eaves providing variable amounts of light, air and privacy to the interior spaces, are said to reflect the gracefulness of a crane's wings as it lands. The pathways allow 70 percent of the roof to be seen from different angles.

LEFT The room in the foreground contains exquisite mother-of-pearl inlay lacquer furniture on its papered floor. The designs depict stories through traditional Korean flora and fauna motifs.

ABOVE All the decorations in the house have meaning. The white plaques attached to posts (bottom left), for example, contain famous quotations from the Chinese classics that serve as reminders to learning and moral behavior.

Mumuheon

House Full of Emptiness

무무헌

Situated on the corner of a street in Gahoe-dong, a neighborhood that used to be the preserve of nobles, scholars and government officials, this house is an example of bringing the past into the present and future. In the mid-1930s, a model house for the Gahoe-dong city *hanok* development was built on the site. Seventy years later, a new *hanok* designed by noted architect Doojin Hwang was erected in its place. Hwang, who has no formal training in traditional Korean architecture, used the project to learn all he could about *hanok* and has since designed some of the most innovative *hanok* in the Bukchon neighborhood.

The name of the house, Mumuheon, or "House Full of Emptiness," perfectly encapsulates the Zen-like ambience of this home in the middle of bustling Seoul. The owner wanted a retreat from the busy world of work, an orthodox design that would create a peaceful space for practicing calligraphy and displaying his art collection. The simplicity of the design, some innovative features and the natural courtyard have helped him achieve his goal. Notably, this is the only house in the book that shows no chairs or beds. The floor is used for relaxing, working, dining and sleeping. Short tables are used when dining and bedding is placed on the heated floor at night.

Built in the style of a city *hanok*, the three sides of the house—the entrance and guest suite along the street side, the long main house opposite the entrance, and the kitchen between them at the far end—form a U shape centered around a courtyard. Three rooms merge into each other in the main house. The *daecheong maru*, or main room, at one end, is the calligraphy area. It has an open southern exposure and is raised slightly higher than the rest of the house to allow a view of roofs and a glimpse of the Seoul skyline. It has a traditional papered wooden floor but with a modern twist: the area under the floor is heated with hot water pipes, not heat from a fire in the kitchen. Adjoining the calligraphy room is a central wood-floored area whose doors face the entrance building, and on the other side of this, the owner's bedroom. All three rooms are replete with the subtle white tones of Korean paper made from natural wood pulp and all are furnished minimally with low tables and chests. Storage space is hidden behind sliding doors, including an attic above the kitchen. In a typical city *hanok*, access to the kitchen is from the courtyard but here several stairs also connect the bedroom with the kitchen. To the left of the kitchen, adjoining the street, is a small bedroom with a bathroom and kitchenette for guests.

PREVIOUS SPREAD The untended courtyard of the house evokes the image of a spacious *hanok* in the countryside. The tiled roofs of the entrance and main house facing each other across the courtyard are capped with decorative eave endings: circular tiles bearing the Chinese character for "longevity" interspersed with curved dripping tiles embellished with an abstract floral motif designed to deflect rainwater from the house, thereby protecting the timber below.

RIGHT The traditional minimal-ist aesthetic of the main house imbues all the rooms with a Zen-like atmosphere that encourages contemplation. Tables and cushions for tea are portable and can be placed anywhere.

OPPOSITE In Korea, pine trees symbolize longevity and steadfastness. A pine in the garden, such as this one near the exterior wall of the courtyard outside the calligraphy room, is thought to bring good luck to the residents of a house.

ABOVE Built nearly ten years ago, the paper floors of the calligraphy room (above left) and guest room (above right) to the left of the kitchen and the wooden floor of the central area have aged naturally, giving them a warm, rustic feel. The owner prefers to practice calligraphy on uncluttered floors, hence the absence of bulky furniture.

ABOVE Traditional Korean paper, one of the most important finishing materials in *hanok*, is glued to all surfaces in the calligraphy room: the floor, walls and ceiling as well as the frames and cross-ribs of the windows. The large paper-covered windows diffuse harsh sunlight to softly bathe the room in natural light, ideal for the art of calligraphy. A tall cabinet holds calligraphy supplies and implements.

RIGHT The rooms in a *hanok* are defined by dividers that can be opened and closed depending on the weather. In winter, dividers close those rooms with heated floors and covered ceilings for thermal efficiency. The unheated central area has a wooden floor and larger openings: doors that lead outside.

ABOVE AND RIGHT In a departure from tradition, small alcoves replace conventional doored wardrobes and are used for displaying the owner's collections of art and antiques in the main bedroom (above) and the guest room (right), which is really two small rooms divided by sliding doors (page 51).

LEFT AND ABOVE LEFT The simplicity and whiteness of the walls and design features of the main bedroom contrast with the ornate details and rich tones visible in the owner's antique collection.

ABOVE Wrapped around the corner of two streets, the house is bordered by a wall of roughly hewn rocks punctuated with entrance steps. The house's sturdy walls, comprising granite blocks at the bottom, a strip of red bricks bearing a simple key fret design of repeating rectangular spirals in the center, and white plaster on top, support the weight of the roof. The flat, rounded dripping tiles along the edge of the roof, placed between the circular end tiles, direct rainwater away from the house, protecting the timber framework.

RIGHT In keeping with tradition, the kitchen (top right) is placed below the level of other rooms in the house, adding to the feel of a country house far from the city. A door behind the kitchen (top right) leads to the guest room. The rubber slippers (bottom right) are rarely used in the city today but are still common in rural areas.

Jamyeongseo

Jamyeong's House of Playing and Reading

자명서실

Located near the end of a quiet alley in Gahoe-dong, this *hanok* was built in 2005 as interest in *hanok* as a contemporary house form began to grow. In developing plans for the house, the owner focused on enjoying the aesthetics of traditional *hanok* and incorporating the spectacular views of the location. Situated on a hill, the house offers what is unique to Seoul, a city surrounded by mountainous ranges.

Like many newly built *hanok* in the first years of the new millennium, this house follows traditional *hanok* aesthetics more closely than recent houses. This trend reflects the interest in traditional, pre-twentieth century aesthetics that accompanied the rediscovery of *hanok* in the late 1990s. The overhangs, for example, are long, extending beyond the walls of the house, which gives them a beautiful traditional curve. In the case of this house, which is primarily constructed of timber, extended eaves also protect the house from the elements.

The house is long, with a *toenmaru*, or wooden terrace, set inside the main part of the building as was common in traditional houses, and wings at each end that extend into the long, narrow courtyard. The wing at the entrance to the house is a formal dining room and the other, at the far end, is a *numaru*, or elevated room, used for tea, surrounded by a veranda. This type of floor plan is more traditional than the enclosed courtyard of a city *hanok*.

The house is one of the first in Gahoe-dong to sit above a semi-basement. Since then, semi-basements, and even fully submerged basements, have become a common way of creating more space while conforming to zoning restrictions aimed at preserving the character of the neighborhood. The exterior wall of the house, which is softened by bamboo, hides the windows of the semi-basement completely.

The house is particularly beautiful at night when the simple lattice windows of the two wings cast a beautiful glow into the courtyard. The long main part of the house in between casts a warm glow as light reflects up from the wooden terrace. The view from the dining room window, meanwhile, shows the night lights of Seoul above the gentle curve of the house below. The prime location of the dining room reflects the owner's idea that a *hanok* is a place for people to gather and share camaraderie in a beautiful setting.

PREVIOUS SPREAD Wood and tile figure prominently in this house, exemplified by the long wooden terrace, with its exterior doors folded and hung up, and the curved tile roof. The soothing colors of nature create a subdued and tranquil yet welcoming atmosphere.

RIGHT The classic *numaru*, or raised room, is a space for entertaining guests or for quiet contemplation. It has latticed windows on three sides of the exterior, typically more ornate than the interior sliding paper-covered screens. Sliding glass panes are sandwiched in between. A latticed door leads to the wooden terrace and the surrounding railed balcony.

LEFT The head sculpture is part of the owner's captivating collection of contemporary art sprinkled throughout the house.

ABOVE The house has tastefully designed modern furniture that suits the traditional Korean floor-sitting lifestyle. As in many renovated *hanok*, the wooden floors in this newly constructed house are warmed using the *ondol* system of under-floor heated water pipes.

LEFT An open multi-purpose shelving unit to the right of the entrance replaces the conventional shoe closet found in most Korean homes, giving the entry contemporary flair. Korea has one of the longest traditions in the world of removing shoes before entering a house and of sitting on the floor for most activities.

RIGHT This corridor, leading to the dining room wing, creates a feeling of space but also helps to insulate the rooms behind it that are closed off with paper-covered doors.

LEFT The dining room, furnished with a sleek contemporary black table, offers a spectacular view of the neighboring *hanok*, downtown Seoul and Mt Namsan beyond. The three layers of window coverings in the room—sliding paper-covered windows in front of sliding glass windows and outer folding lattices—diffuse harsh sunlight in summer and keep out drafts in winter.

ABOVE A contemporary sculpture at one end of the dining room table contrasts with the symmetry of the framed window view of the courtyard, terrace and *numaru* wing.

ABOVE Contemporary art provides color and surprise against the subtle white and earth tones typical of a *hanok*.

OPPOSITE Small traditional rooms (bottom right) that look as though they were built in the nineteenth century, contrast with the contemporary designer bathroom (above right and bottom left). Sliding paper-covered doors link each room. The vertical and horizontal lines that dominate the design of traditional rooms contribute to their simplicity and tranquility.

LEFT The long wooden terrace acts as an intermediate space between the house and courtyard. Managing a southern exposure is important in *hanok*. The broad eaves keep the sun out in summer but allow it to warm the terrace and walls of the house in winter. Exquisite craftsmanship and attention to detail are the hallmarks of this house.

ABOVE The combination granite block and brick wall and small tile-roofed gate (top left and right), which mimicks the curve of the house roof, contribute to the low profile of the house along the alley, helping it blend into the neighborhood. The artistry of the woodworking and complexity of the roof structure are apparent in the balcony of the elevated wing (bottom left) and corner eaves outside the dining wing (bottom right).

Jiwuheon

House of Continuous Learning

지우헌

Located at the top of the hill in Gahoe-dong, this house, built in 2011, combines traditional Korean architecture and contemporary features to create an integrated whole. As a leading figure in the field of design in Korea, the owner has a deep love and appreciation of traditional Korean architecture and craftsmanship and her efforts in raising awareness of and promoting good design in Korea have helped turn the country into the competitive design powerhouse that it is today.

To her, craftsmanship is critical to good design. She built her *hanok* to show her support for traditional craftsmanship and to help preserve it for future generations. Building a *hanok* involves a number of specialized trade skills: woodwork, stonework, brickwork, metalwork, roof tiling and, of course, paper making. If *hanok* were not built, these skilled artisans would be out of a job and their craft would not be passed to their apprentices and down the generations.

The design of the exterior spaces of the house is unconventional for a *hanok*. From the traditional tile-capped main gate, a set of stairs to the right leads up to a small paved courtyard that sits between the two protruding wings of the house. A glass roof over the courtyard allows it to be used on rainy days.

From the entrance to the house, another set of stairs leads down to a large area under the main body of the house, much like a sunken garden. To the right of this sunken area is the entrance to the semi-basement, which contains a multimedia room with a raised platform on which the owner practices *pansori*, a Korean genre of musical storytelling performed by a vocalist and a drummer. Directly in front of the stairs is a raised wooden floor with a low wooden table down the center, one end supported on a large stone. The platform-like floor is a cool sitting area for entertaining in the hot summer months.

Because of the owner's interest in design and craftsmanship, the house has a number of time-honored details rarely seen in renovated *hanok*. For example, some of the papered closet doors have traditional-style paintings of flowers, birds and insects on them, adding a decorative touch to the minimalist *hanok* interior. Moreover, the posts on the parts of the house facing the courtyard are adorned with white *juryeon*, or post plaques, carved with sayings, most commonly in classical Chinese, which express the wishes and tastes of the owner.

PREVIOUS SPREAD This decorative clay wall embraces the side and back of the sunken garden, forming a wonderfully cool space for outdoor activities on a hot summer day.

RIGHT A classic wooden tea room, slightly elevated above the main house and extending out from it, is a quiet and private part of the house, which is itself set slightly below ground level. A low-railed narrow balcony runs in front of the windows.

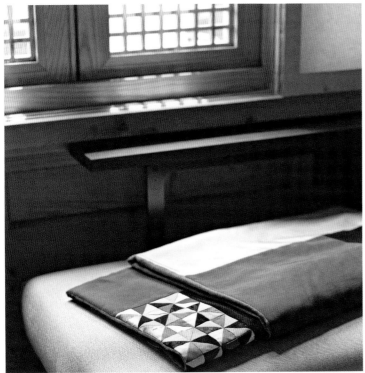

OPPOSITE In keeping with Korean tradition, spaces in the house have different functions. A wide hall, for example, has been turned into an open space for writing and studying.

ABOVE The owner of the house is a connoisseur of traditional Korean arts and crafts, reflected in such items as the silk bedspread made using old quilting techniques, the writing brushes made by traditional brush maker Pilmu Yu (each takes 2–3 months to make from natural materials) and the rigid oval hand fan.

LEFT A stone statue of a tiger by artist Chehyun Oh and a pot plant in a ceramic bowl adorn the second entrance to the house. Plants soften the starkness of the wall behind.

LEFT AND ABOVE The dining room and adjoining kitchen occupy a large area that allows for friendly informal gatherings amid the elegance of an open *hanok* ceiling. The imaginative twig-covered light fixture above the long wooden table was specially commissioned for the dining area.

FOLLOWING SPREAD The long, narrow window in the kitchen not only provides privacy but evokes a traditional Korean ink painting in the way it frames the undulating roof lines of the neighboring houses. The contemporary red lacquer cabinet, made by lacquer expert Yongbok Jeon, draws on the tradition of fine lacquer furniture in Korea. The natural lacquer is resistant to humidity and insects as well as being waterproof.

OPPOSITE The bedroom seamlessly mixes traditional *hanok* aesthetics, such as the varnished paper floor, with contemporary Western-style furniture.

THIS PAGE Compared to many other *hanok*, the house includes a number of modern conveniences, such as built-in vanities, alongside traditional artifacts like the floor cushions and low lacquered table.

LEFT AND ABOVE With its multiple layers of windows and doors open in summer, the tea room lets the outside in, but in winter can be turned into an intimate closed space. *Hanok* doors are made in sets of two, four, six or eight. In the four-set doors in this tea room, the two center doors are pulled to each side. A low-railed balcony decorated with a simple grid design surrounds three sides of the tea room. Designed by furniture and light designer Donghui Hong, the tea room table is formed from a large slab of treated old wood, supported at one end by a wooden leg and at the other by a large stone. The wood and stone combination adds a touch of rusticity to the refined environment of the *hanok*.

LEFT AND RIGHT The open sitting space under the house, reached by a set of stairs near the entrance, evokes the scale of a country estate and is a perfect setting for traditional Korean musical performances. The sturdy posts supporting the roof are set on stone bases (right) to prevent rotting from contact with soil or water. The paneled ceiling (above) is a rare example of this type of traditional ceiling in a contemporary *hanok*. Here, as in the tea room, one end of the rustic table, designed by Donhui Hong, is supported by a stone. The roll-down fabric blinds are used for privacy and give the space a small, more intimate feeling.

LEFT The juxtaposition of traditional Korean tea room and modern patio with glass roof (see page 13, center) and all-weather Western-style furniture illustrates how many preservation-minded Koreans have embraced a mix of old and new for modern living. The complexity of the entrance gate roof is apparent from the room and patio.

ABOVE The tile-capped entrance gate (top left) flanked by a combination granite block and brick wall reflects the architecture of the *hanok* behind. Tableware in the tea room ranges from a traditional iron stove and kettle (bottom left) to a modern white ceramic tea set (top right). A contemporary floral decoration (bottom right) adds color to the dining area.

Simsimheon

House Where the Heart is Found

심심헌

Sitting on the main street in Gahoe-dong, this *hanok* pays homage to traditional Korean aesthetics. The owner is active in neighborhood affairs and welcomes neighbors into her home for discussions on local concerns. She also opens the house to the public on weekends as a way of promoting a deeper understanding of *hanok*. The name of the house, "Simsimheon," is a play on words that reflect the owner's openness toward others. The literal meaning is "a house for collecting your mind" but the word *simsim* also means "to be at a loose end," a metaphorical invitation for people to drop by whenever they are free.

The house, which is set above a fully submerged basement, is shaped like the Korean letter *giyeok* (ㄱ), with a large, ornate *numaru*, or elevated room, that projects southward. The main room, the *daecheong maru* at right angles to it, opens on two sides and offers stunning views of Seoul on one side and the large courtyard on the other. The courtyard itself is interesting because it contains two pine trees, which extend the metaphor of relaxation implied by the name of the house. Traditionally, pines were not planted inside an estate because it was thought they would make the people who lived there lazy. Here, they are an invitation to relax and get away from the world of work.

As the owner spent some time in Latin America, she wanted the *hanok* to reflect her time there. The house has a warm feeling, be it from the sun, wood or tiles. The wood, inside and out, casts a warm tone, and the basement, which is not visible from the outside, also has a cozy atmosphere. A space between the interior and exterior walls of the basement prevents it from developing a musty smell, an important architectural innovation.

The house has a number of details that reflect the owner's love of *hanok*. The narrow balcony around the *numaru* has an ornately carved railing. The doors to the wood-floored *daecheong maru* fold up and can be hung from the ceiling in the traditional way of opening up the house to the outside in warm weather. The paper on the doors to the bedroom has been treated in the traditional way with oil to strengthen it, which also gives it a special glow in the light. Some of the large cross beams in the house are exquisite pieces of antique wood salvaged from larger *hanok* that have been demolished.

Although the house is a new construction, it fits in seamlessly with the Gahoe-dong streetscape. The pattern of the band of bricks above the stones on the exterior wall creates a warm image, which foreshadows the interior. By mixing hints of Latin-inspired warm tones with traditional Korean architecture, this house creates a sensibility all of its own.

PREVIOUS SPREAD The pine trees, open doors and grass, all a rarity in densely populated Seoul, create a sanctuary in the center of the city.

RIGHT The heated rooms with varnished paper floors are small, in keeping with the Korean tradition of conserving energy in winter.

LEFT The view from the terrace of the main room shows how the house embraces the contours of the sloping site. In the background, the high-rise buildings of central Seoul are in complete architectural contrast to this beautiful oasis of calm.

ABOVE In Korean, the word for window and door is the same because windows, such as those in this little tea room, can also be used as doors.

LEFT The Goryeo Period (918–1392) ceramics on top of the mother-of-pearl inlay lacquer ware table in the main room pay homage to the understated but powerful beauty of Korean art.

RIGHT The owner collects a variety of antique Korean ceramics, including pieces that were used by commoners, such as the small black pot on a low chest in the tea room.

OPPOSITE Painting the ends of exposed rafters white became popular in the twentieth century but traditionally, as shown here, they were left untouched.

ABOVE The house has a number of details that older Koreans remember from their childhood, such as the colorful quilted bedding (top right) and the black rubber shoes (bottom right).

Seonyudang

House of Sharing and Kindness

선유당

This is an interesting example of a mid-sized city *hanok* that feels bigger than it actually is. Located on a picturesque street near Gye-dong, the house was first renovated in 2006 and became known to passersbys for its dark wood and playful brick design. The current owner renovated the house in 2012 for use as a living-cum-work space. She hired Guga Urban Architecture, a firm founded by the noted architect Junggoo Cho. Since the early 2000s, Cho has taken the lead in a number of restoration and new construction projects throughout Korea, merging contemporary needs with traditional *hanok*.

The owner, who runs a cultural foundation, wanted a home that projected an open and welcoming image. To create a feeling of space, the architect opened up the house by removing fixed internal walls and by installing floor-to-ceiling picture windows to take advantage of the spectacular view of Mt Inwangsan to the west. The view through the windows is of rows of *hanok* and their curving roofs. Taking the idea of "borrowed scenery" a step further, the glass ceiling-height window in the courtyard offers an unobstructed view to the entrance.

With the internal walls removed, the ceiling, already high compared to other city *hanok*, adds to the open feel of the house The long part of the house has a southern exposure and natural light flows to all parts of the house. The combination of space, light and outside views creates an open atmosphere that is difficult to find in other *hanok*. The openness of the house also highlights the warm beauty of the wood, an important reminder of the importance of wood in *hanok* aesthetics.

To make the best use of the available space, the house has an abundance of built-in storage. Some of the kitchen fixtures are mounted on casters, allowing them to be pulled out when needed, which opens up the space above for storage. In the *deacheong maru*, or main room, tables for tea are stored in a narrow space between the wall and the floor, becoming a shelf when stored. Outside, the lower stone walls of the exterior protrude more than usual to accommodate bookshelves hidden behind sliding doors.

In the hands of an owner and an architect who both love and appreciate *hanok*, this house has become a bright, warm space that celebrates openness and the beauty of borrowed scenery.

PREVIOUS SPREAD Both the sun and a heated wood floor warm the main room in winter. Previously, traditional wood floors were not heated, only papered ones, but new technology has made this possible. The doors on the right open out to a narrow courtyard, extending the living space in the warmer months.

RIGHT The trees beyond the front entrance, which are located on a nearby wooded hill on the other side of the street, perform the function of the Japanese-derived concept of "borrowed scenery," bringing more of nature into the house. The small room next to the entrance, which has an unusual wooden bench for guests, is used as a reception room or for displays.

ABOVE AND LEFT Floor-heated rooms in a *hanok*, like this one, are generally small in order to conserve energy in the winter months. The large windows and sliding door (above), with a half-wall behind for privacy, make an interesting contrast to the rhythmic curves of the tiled roofs visible at eye level from the room. A tasteful mix of antique and contemporary furniture (right) gives the room a modern, urban feel.

THIS PAGE AND RIGHT Most small *hanok* lack adequate storage space but this one is an exception. Things are kept organized with clever storage ideas, such as the narrow shelves below the exterior windows (top left) and the built-in cupboards surrounding an alcove (right). The copper sink in the bathroom (above) evokes the tradition of handcrafted Korean metalwork, a common feature of traditional *hanok*. The courtyard (left) leading off the main room extends the living space and allows furniture, such as this striking red armchair and white table, to be kept outside in fine weather.

LEFT AND ABOVE Pot gardens used to be common in older neighborhoods in Seoul. The pot garden in this courtyard plays on that history and allows the plants to be moved for sun and shade as needed. The simple, undecorated wall behind the courtyard adds to the bright feeling of the house and harmonizes with its contemporary features and furnishings.

Bansongjae

Studio Cherishing an Old Pine Tree
as a Lifelong Friend

반송재

Hugging the side of a hill in Samcheong-dong, this house was completed in 2010 with the help of Moonho Lee, a local architect trained in traditional architecture. Surrounded by sturdy granite walls, the house comprises two conjoined *hanok*, each about 150 square meters with its own 50-square meter garden above two new semi-basements, added to provide the necessary space for work and living. The former director of the National Museum of Korea lives here and continues her work as one of Korea's leading art historians through a research institute that operates in part of the house. The upper house, or *sarangchae*, is mostly for guests and entertaining and the lower house, *or anchae*, contains her private living quarters and library. The functional division of the houses reflects the traditional division of space in Korean houses between men's quarters where men welcomed guests and women's quarters where women cooked and raised children.

The owner's passion for *hanok* goes back to the mid-1990s when she led a project to restore architecturally important *hanok* in the southern part of Korea. After finishing that project, she turned her attention to *hanok* in Bukchon and became an important voice in calling for preservation of the area. She poured years of experience into this house and it shows clearly in the details. The upper house, for example, has an elevated room with a wooden floor. Known as a *numaru*, the small room has windows that open outward on three sides, capturing stunning views of Mt Inwangsan to the west.

The outstanding feature of the house are its proportions. Critical to *hanok* aesthetics is an elegant balance between the height of the building and the length of the eaves. City *hanok* of the 1930s compromised this aesthetic because of the lack of space, but this house recreates the beauty of a traditional *hanok* estate through proportion and spacing between the buildings.

The research institute in the semi-basement of the lower house, which has a separate entrance from the street, is full of thousands of art books, research materials and the owner's collection of antiques. The semi-basement in the upper house is one large open living area with Western-style furniture and plenty of space in which to relax and entertain guests, and a pristine white kitchen. Because it is sited one level higher, it receives light from the courtyard of the lower house.

PREVIOUS SPREAD This elevated room, or *numaru*, in the upper house has a splendid view through its latticed windows of Mt Inwangsan, one of Seoul's most beloved mountains.

RIGHT The semi-basement of the upper house has a large bright living and entertaining space. A stunning talking point is the armchair designed by well-known Canadian-American architect/designer Frank Gehry from his 1970s cardboard furniture series "Easy Edges."

LEFT The painting above the window of the *numaru* of the lower house is how Seon Jeong (1676–1759), one of Korea's most famous landscape painters, perceived Mt Inwangsan, which appears in full view through the window. The *numaru* is connected to the owner's bedroom.

RIGHT Composed of two small *hanok* connected to make one, the reconstructed house has many small spaces, such as this exterior walkway in the upper house.

FOLLOWING SPREAD The modern semi-basement of the upper house is a multi-purpose space for relaxing and entertaining guests.

OPPOSITE Despite the small spaces, the lack of buildings surrounding the house allows light to come in, which subtly enhances the owner's collections of hair combs and weaving shuttles, among other items. The bedroom of the lower house (top right) has paper-covered glass windows.

ABOVE The owner lives and works in the house, which gives it a friendly, lived-in look, such as this room in the upper house. Many of the modern amenities inside the house are shielded from view by wood-framed lattice doors.

LEFT AND THIS PAGE Open latticed doors of the wood-floored main room of the upper house (left) frame a lovely view of the courtyard, which is gently shaded by a gnarled pine tree. Interesting artifacts, such as an old mortar (below right), are dotted around the sand garden of the upper house. The owner likes to relax by making small crafts from wood left over from the construction of the house, such as the flowers on the balcony of the upper house *numaru* (above right). Her workroom, with a workbench and tools (above left), is located in the main room of the lower house.

Moto Hano

Moto House

모토한옥

Situated on a quiet street in Samcheong-dong that tourists have yet to discover, this house is a robust if not idiosyncratic example of a mixed *hanok*. The owner/architect who designed the renovations wanted to create a playful space that his family could enjoy and grow up in. Like most other *hanok* in Bukchon, the house was originally built in the 1930s as part of a city *hanok* development project. The houses in the Samcheong-dong district were more modest than the ones in neighboring Gahoe-dong.

The lifting of building restrictions in the 1990s allowed several modern buildings to be constructed nearby. To block these from view, the owner raised the level of the courtyard area so that the line of vision went above the modern structures. Because he also needed more space for his family, he created a full-height basement. The raised courtyard allows for a high ceiling in the living areas. A skylight set into the deck, with mirrors on all sides, reflects light down into the basement and adds to the impression of space. A small sitting space above the kitchen offers views of the house, the neighborhood, downtown Seoul to the south and Gyeongbokgung Palace and Mt Inwangsan to the west.

In addition to playing with layers and viewpoints, the owner/architect also played with light and color. The kitchen cabinets and much of the rest of the house are a bright yellow green, which produces a warm, Latin feel. The owner chose green because it represents bamboo, which is an important motif in traditional Korean ink painting. The exterior wall has a window with a mesh made of roof tiles in front of it that lets light into the living area, while the kitchen gets light from skylights that fill the area between the roof and the exterior wall. The kitchen, which is next to the entrance, was designed to be the center of the house, a reflection of the owner's Italian heritage. His father was also an architect and his childhood home was one with no doors. It was natural that he incorporate this open-space concept into his own home.

Most of the *hanok* renovations that began in the early years of this century focused on turning 1930s city *hanok* into comfortable houses imbued with the aesthetics of a traditional rural estate. This house goes in the opposite direction by creating a truly contemporary space that brings the city *hanok* into the twenty-first century.

PREVIOUS SPREAD The traditional *hanok* gate opens to a dramatic interior with Mediterranean flair.

RIGHT The house is full of open spaces that keep the family in touch with each other. The big red-framed mirror in the living room allows the parents in the kitchen to keep an eye on what their young children are doing.

OPPOSITE The courtyard has become a deck for outdoor playing and entertaining. Built-in wooden seating borders the deck. Bicycles are suspended from wall brackets below the roof eaves, keeping them out of the way as well as protecting them from the elements.

ABOVE The conversation pit in the living area was designed so that all that could be seen at eye level was the tiled roof of the house next door. The taller modern building in the distance is barely visible.

OPPOSITE AND THIS PAGE This is a fun house with a fascinating mix of conventional and innovative spaces for living, working and playing, all harmoniously linked by the bright green color scheme running through the house.

130

ABOVE Skylights at the entrance and in the floor of the deck as well as narrow windows running below the outer edges of the ceiling let light into the basement and above-ground rooms. In addition to the wooden outdoor deck with its built-in seating (top right), a small patio above the kitchen allows views of the neighborhood and beyond.

OPPOSITE The glass walls surrounding the courtyard-cum-deck create a "glass *hanok*" à la Philip Johnson, the influential American architect famed for his use of glass and his own Glass House residence in Connecticut.

Cheongsongjae and Neungsoheon

House of a Green Pine Tree and Trumpet Vine

청송재 와 능소헌

Located just off the artsy main street in Gye-dong in Bukchon, this is one of the very few *hanok* that have been renovated twice. Built in the late 1920s, the house is an early example of the emerging city *hanok* style. To create a larger space, two houses were combined into one during the first renovation, in 1997. Both houses, upper and lower, are shaped like the letter *mieum* (ㅁ) but the upper differs in having an opening in the top right corner.

The current owner, an interior designer, renovated the conjoined house in 2012 to suit his personal taste, which reflects the sensibilities of a new generation of Koreans who move effortlessly between Korean and Western culture. The result is an interior that encompasses the visual angles of an older city *hanok* while creating a contemporary, almost hip, ambience. The formal dining room in the upper house, for example, combines the aesthetics of traditional beams with a modern ceiling and post-World War II minimalist Danish furniture. Likewise, the living room combines a traditional exposed beam ceiling with a cutting-edge ethanol-burning fireplace.

The upper house serves as both a living and work space for the owner whose office is located in what was once the *daecheong maru*, or main room. The office is flooded with natural light and has views of a small garden to the north and the *madang*, or courtyard, to the south. Parts of the courtyard contain moss gardens that surround a few stately pine trees, whereas other parts are paved with cut stone.

During his childhood, the owner and his mother frequented Insa-dong, Seoul's antique district, on weekends. He credits his interest in design to these visits, and a number of objects he collected there are displayed around in the house. One of his favorites, and the inspiration for his *hanok*, is a figurine of a fictional Chinese animal whose spirit protects the house. After moving in, he gave the figurine a permanent home by placing it on one of the roof tiles in the upper house.

The lower house, where his parents live, is connected to the upper house by a narrow, almost hidden, passage. That house also has moss and pine trees in its courtyard around which the elegant design of the latticed windows from the 1997 renovation is on glorious display. In the 2012 renovation, the owner took great care to maintain the integrity of the original houses as a testament to the past while adding modern amenities not hinted at from the exterior. The layer of renovation and mix of uses give new meaning to the concept of mixed *hanok*.

PREVIOUS SPREAD The focal point of the upper house courtyard, which is paved in concrete slabs, is a small water basin for water lilies carved from a single stone, placed on a moss-covered mound.

RIGHT Tasteful contemporary furnishings are entirely compatible with the traditional *hanok*-style wooden pillars, beams, rafters, doors, windows and flooring in the living room of the upper house.

LEFT Traditionally, *hanok* courtyards are left open and become an "exterior living space" but in this house they have been turned into decorative gardens. Gutters along the edges of the shortened eaves, typical of city *hanok*, catch rainwater to prevent it damaging the timber structure below.

ABOVE Wide sliding doors open the living room to the outside and make the small room feel bigger.

RIGHT The mixture of stone, moss and pine trees in the courtyard draws on the iconography of traditional Korean ink painting.

ABOVE The pine trees in the courtyard garden are reminiscent of a mountain village far from Seoul. Surrounded by nature and an open sky, the *hanok* is a soothing and inspirational place in which to live and work.

RIGHT Modernity again meets tradition in this guest bedroom. The creative use of color and a simple headboard and bedding accentuate the gently curving ceiling and collection of traditional Korean painting and calligraphy.

LEFT AND RIGHT The small home office under a handsome ceiling in the former *daecheong maru*, or main room, of the upper house is divided by a glass partition into a private work space for the owner and a meeting place for clients and colleagues. The whiteness of the walls and paper-covered windows is offset by the blue-and-white ceramics on the glass shelves, designed by Teo Yang and manufactured in Thailand, and the colorful figures on the floor.

LEFT The elegant dining room, complete with vintage rosewood table, has a practical Carrara marble tiled floor. The air-conditioning unit above the mirrored storage cupboard on the right is hidden behind wooden slats. The tableware and lamps on the buffet against the far wall were designed by Teo Yang.

RIGHT For older Koreans, this small guest room evokes memories of the small bedrooms they grew up with. The attached bathroom at the end is a practical contemporary touch.

FOLLOWING SPREAD The garden in the courtyard of the lower house helps break up a large symmetrical space and makes it feel more intimate.

THIS PAGE The owner is fond of plants, which are found even in the smallest of places throughout the house, including eight small courtyards. The courtyard-cum-dining area at top left is located off the hall that leads from the living room to the owner's bedroom. The dark pots on the structure behind the steps are called *onggi* and are the traditional way of storing *kimchi* and other condiments. The fish-painted ceramics (above right), known as Haeju pots, are from North Korea's Hwanghac Province and were made toward the end of the Joseon Dynasty.

RIGHT The layered roofs of the upper and lower houses are covered with the original roof tiles, which create a fascinating mosaic of earth tones. Trees peep through the two exposed courtyards.

Changseongdong Jip

House in Changseong-dong

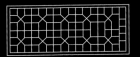

창송동집

The cliché "good things come in small packages" is an apt description of this contemporary city *hanok* designed by owner/architect Seungmo Seo. Located in Changseong-dong in the Seochon area of Seoul, the house is an excellent example of how a small *hanok* can be remodeled to suit a contemporary lifestyle. Seochon is located on the opposite side of the Gyeongbokgung Palace from its more famous cousin Bukchon. The *hanok* in Seochon are smaller than in Bukchon and there was far less mass-scale *hanok* development in the 1930s.

Because many houses in Seochon are small, the challenge is how to make the best use of the given space. The owner first became interested in *hanok* because its unique form offered a number of architectural challenges. With this house, he decided to shrink the size of the *madang*, or courtyard, and turn what remained into a "light box." This shifted the living space closer to the courtyard garden, which allowed him to shorten the overhangs and allow more light to penetrate the house. Along many of the exterior walls, he placed built-in closets and storage space. The kitchen is small but with all modern conveniences as the owner is an avid cook. There is ample built-in storage so the kitchen is easy to navigate and does not look crowded. The home has evolved and changed from the time of the initial renovation when the owner was a bachelor to when he became a husband and father.

A unique feature of the house is a long glass passageway linking what was once part of the courtyard. Though the passage is not living space, it gives balance to the courtyard by echoing the glass wall in the living room. With glass walls on three sides and concrete on the ground, the courtyard evokes the inverse image of Philip Johnson's glass house. The owner likes light and he created and added a triangular hood to the narrow southward-facing window to capture light and reflect it down into the passage.

Another distinctive trait of the owner's work is the juxtaposition of old and new. Aside from the aesthetic appeal of *hanok*, embracing the old helps reduce costs and allows them to be renovated in stages as budgets permit. Most *hanok* are renovated in complete gut renovations but the owner took his time with this house and decided to leave the exterior as it was. From the outside, the house looks like another aging city *hanok* in Seochon except for the large white contemporary door, a contrast that makes passersby wonder what is behind it. Contemporary flair mixed with respect for the old combine to make this house distinctive among city *hanok*.

PREVIOUS SPREAD A brushed aluminum and leather lounger and ottoman designed by Charles Eames set the tone for this small contemporary *hanok*. The silver-gray Chinese granite floor tiles used throughout the house optically enlarge the open plan.

RIGHT The extent of the original courtyard has been reduced to create more living space, though it continues to function as the main source of light and air entering the house. Stacks of books and magazines demarcate the living and dining areas.

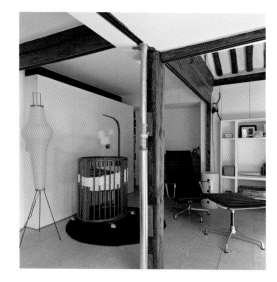 

ABOVE The house makes use of the classic architectural trick of constrained spaces opening into larger spaces (above right). This creates a sense of surprise that makes the house feel bigger. The kitchen (above left), though small, has air-conditioning, sleek kitchen appliances and ample storage in cupboards or on fitted shelves.

OPPOSITE This view from the kitchen into the dining room illustrates how built-in storage, including open shelving, helps keep a small space free of clutter.

LEFT The only enclosed room in the house is the bathroom. In a radical departure from tradition, in which small rooms are the norm, the rest of the house is one large open plan divided into specific areas by furniture.

ABOVE The architect, who is also an avid cook, has made space for an intimate dining area with a retro mid-twentieth century feel.

Hwadongjae

House of Becoming One with Others

화동재

Located on a picturesque site in the village of Joanni, this is the only house in the book not in a dense urban setting. At first glance, the pastoral location makes it the most traditional house in the book, but its modern wing, though clothed in a traditional exterior and sited at the foot of an old *hanok*, turns the house into a mix of old and new.

The entrance to the house is through the modern wing, which consists of three separate buildings: a kitchen, bath house and two-storied living room, bedroom and study. The entrance is a narrow passage between the bath house and living room, which opens into a long courtyard that echoes those of city *hanok*. A path from the courtyard leads through vegetation and up a small hill to where the *hanok* sits.

The *hanok* is also small but the wood is of the highest quality, which gives it a delicate tone. The interior is minimalist and follows traditional aesthetics rigidly. In keeping with the need to conserve heat, the floor-heated *ondol* rooms are small, with thick lacquered paper on the floors and milky white Korean paper on the walls. The house has a spacious *numaru*, or elevated room, with a wooden floor, and a windowless enclosed porch at the end. In warm weather, the room can be opened to the porch creating a large space that is open to nature.

The owner uses the house as a second home, and thus the space is organized around the need to relax and enjoy time with family and guests. The family spends most of its time in the modern wing. Here, the kitchen and living room are bright and open to encourage people to gather and talk. The large windows have views of the garden and, from the kitchen, the *hanok* on the hill.

At every turn, the contrasts in the house—traditional versus modern, formal versus casual, refined versus rustic—create a stimulating mix that offers new perspectives. Because the two buildings are detached, people are brought in touch with nature as they move from one to the other. The separation of the *hanok* from the functional living space also liberates it from the need to be modern, thus allowing it to retain its traditional roots.

PREVIOUS SPREAD With its dark wood and roof tiles, this house feels like a natural part of the Korean countryside.

RIGHT Traditionally, Korean houses have little decoration on the walls and minimal furniture. The resulting simplicity was thought to help clear the mind for study and contemplation.

ABOVE Modern conveniences in the new wing, such as wash basins, storage and a small kitchen holding items for the tea ceremony, are hidden from view in closets that give the impression of being doors leading to another room.

OPPOSITE High quality fully dried wood is difficult to obtain in Korea but the wood in this house has an unusually rich color and shows no signs of cracking or warping. The rack on the wall of this room was formerly used for storing dry calligraphy brushes.

LEFT A stack of traditional Korean rectangular pillows is a marvelous talking point in the living room of the new wing. The pillows have square padded ends embellished with intricate, vibrant embroidery, typically related to symbols of good fortune and longevity. Embroidery is also used to decorate screens, sitting cushions and bedding covers.

RIGHT Known as *baduk* in Korea, this simple wood Go game set helps family members and visitors enjoy relaxing analog play.

FOLLOWING SPREAD The *numaru* of the *hanok* (right) floats high above ground, creating a dramatic space for relaxation or entertainment. The recessed collonade-like space (left) is typical of large old *hanok* in the countryside. The rectangular stepping stones in front indicate entrances and are used for placing shoes while inside the house.

ABOVE The contemporary wing of the house has open yet simple spaces with beautiful wood highlights. The spacious bath house (above left), in a separate building, allows for family bathing as is common in hot springs in Korea, especially for fun bath times for the grandchildren. The dining area (above right) is an extension of the open-plan kitchen.

OPPOSITE The walk from the *hanok* to the contemporary wing goes through trees that hide the contemporary wing from view. The bath house is on the left.

FOLLOWING SPREAD As the spiritual heart of the house, the kitchen invites people to gather and mingle over relaxing meals. Designed by Songryong Cho, the ceiling is made of pine wood planks and the cabinets, countertop and sink are by Italian kitchen specialist Boffi.

ABOVE, CLOCKWISE FROM TOP LEFT Chimneys are no longer used in city *hanok* where pipes carrying hot water heat the floors, but this one is part of the traditional wood-burning system used to heat the *hanok* wing. A corner of the *hanok* veranda railing, a collage-like granite wall and a sunken stone mortar under the balcony of the *hanok* exemplify the long-established taste and artistry of Korean designers and artisans.

OPPOSITE Surrounded by trees, the house's new wing, built in the 2000s, looks as if it has been there for centuries.

Acknowledgments

This book would not have have been published without the generous support of many individuals and institutions.

First and foremost, I would like to thank the owners of the twelve wonderful *hanok* that are featured for their generosity in opening up their homes and sharing their stories with us. Their participation in the project is at the very heart of this book.

I am especially grateful to photographer Jongkeun Lee and his assistants Seongbeom Heo and Mineun Kim for their artistry as well as their patience and perseverance in the face of unpredictable weather and other unavoidable circumstances. When I look at the photographs in the book, I am speechless. They truly capture the soul of these homes and bring them to life.

I am also thankful to Robert J. Fouser. Robert was able to bring many insights to the book and to highlight the details of the twelve homes that are featured. His introduction to the book sets the scene from both an historical and architectural viewpoint.

Further thanks go to the Arumjigi Culture Keeper Foundation, the National Trust of Korea and the YEOL Korea Heritage Preservation Society for their guidance. To all of the architects, *hanok* specialists, designers and historians who have become friends along the way, I owe a special thanks for guidance and advice. They have inspired me to continue sharing our heritage and culture with the rest of the world.

I would also like to extend a special thanks to Eric Oey and Christina Ong of Tuttle Publishing for believing in me and trusting my vision for this book. A big thank you also goes to June Chong and Chan Sow Yun of Tuttle Publishing for organizing a design and layout that beautifully weaves pictures and words, and Song Hui Choi and Noor Azlina Yunus for their editorial input.

Last but not least, I would like to thank my *ohana* (family) and friends for their patience and support. This book would not have been possible without them!

Thank you all very much! *Gomapsumnida! Mahalo nui loa!*

—**Nani Park**

Designers and Architects

Simone CARENA

MOTOElastico
Best Italian Architecture office in Korea
Jongno-gu 5ga 4th floor, Seoul,
Korea 110-836
Tel: 82-2-542-9298
www.motoelastico.com

Simone Carena was born in Torino, Italy. He currently divides his time between Seoul and Torino with his wife, fashion designer Jihye Shin, and their two sons, Felice and Forte. He is Assistant Professor of Digital Media and Space Design at IDAS, Hongik University, Director and Founder of the IDAS Smart City Lab in cooperation with the MIT Senseable City Lab, and Director of the Brain Korea 21 Plus Program (BK21 Plus) International between Hongik University, Kingston University London and MIT Boston.

Carena holds a Master of Architecture from the Southern California Institute of Architecture, USA, and a Master of Architecture with Honors from Politecnico di Torino, Italy. He did further studies in architecture and design at Harvard Graduate Design School in the US and Oxford Polytechnic University, UK.

MOTOElastico in an experimental space-lab working on architecture, design and art projects whose goal is to challenge local cultures through unexpected combinations of original ingredients. MOTOElastico means "harmonic motion" and overlaps with the dynamics of orbits. The firm offers "a dynamic view of the body we orbit. We never land, but we exchange visitors and data with the surface." The company was founded with Marco Bruno, the Best Italian Architecture Office in Korea. Together with Marco Bruno and Minji Kim, Carena is the author of *Borrowed City*, based on the way private citizens use public space in Seoul, and the recipient of several awards. MOTOElastico won the Golden Lion Award for the best pavilion at the Venice Architecture Biennale 2014.

Junggoo CHO

Guga Urban Architecture
16-3 Jongro-gu Gahoe-dong, Seoul Korea
Tel: 82-2-3789-3372; Fax: 82-2-3789-3373
gugaua@hanmail.net /www.guga.co.kr

Junggoo Cho, born in 1966, earned his BS and MA degrees in architecture at Seoul National University and was a doctoral candidate at the University of Tokyo. In 2002, he established Guga Urban Architecture. Focusing on "ordinary architecture related to our life," Guga is involved in an ongoing urban research project, "Wednesday Survey," and the restoration and refurbishment of *hanok*. The purpose of "Wednesday Survey" is to explore, observe and record in detail old residential neighborhoods and buildings in Seoul that are rapidly being demolished and redeveloped. Since the first Wednesday research trip in 2000, the program is now headed towards its 670th. Guga is gradually expanding its research boundary to several other residential areas and urban planning projects in Seoul.

Since its first *hanok* project in 2001, the firm has worked on large- and small-scale *hanok* in the Bukchon area where it has looked for diverse modern *hanok* forms that embrace a modern lifestyle. The accumulated effort of many years is shown in the *hanok* hotel Ragung which received first prize in the 2007 Korea Wood Design Awards. Under the idea of modern evolution, Guga is working on many projects within the traditional range.

Misook CHYUNG

Korea Furniture Museum, Seoul
330-5777 Seongbuk-dong, Seongbuk-gu,
Seoul, Korea
Tel: 82-2-745-0181
www.kofum.com

Misook Chyung has a BFA and MFA from Ewha Womans University. She also studied at Istanbul University, at the National Folklore Museum in Denmark and at the Design School, Art Institute of Seattle, USA.

In 1993, former professor Chyung founded the Korea Furniture Museum and assumed the role of Director. It took almost fifteen years to build the ten new *hanok* structures in different styles in the grounds of the private museum where many of the 2,500 pieces of traditional wooden furniture and household goods made from the Joseon Dynasty, which she personally amassed over five decades, are housed. Through her vision and tireless effort, the museum has become a world-renowned repository of furniture that gives an insight into the interior decoration and traditional lifestyles of old Korea.

Other than the permanent exhibition, Chyung has organized special exhibitions of Korean Folk Art painting and a special archival exhibit with Gucci, both featuring traditional Korean furniture and lifestyles under director Chyung's curation. She has also organized a Korean cultural program, Seongbuk-Seowon Academy, for the spouses of foreign ambassadors to Korea and expatriate CEOs in Seoul, which offers an introduction to traditional Korean heritage, including its architecture, cuisine, clothing and way of life.

Misook Chyung was an advisor for the interior of the presidential palace ("Blue House") and the construction of over fifty traditional Korean houses in Seoul. In 2009, she won the Acheon Prize from the Korean Institute of Architects, which is awarded for buildings that best reflect design principles unique to Korea and traditional Korean aesthetics. Currently, she is a member of the Citizens Committee for Urban Renaissance for Seoul, the Advisory Committee in the diplomatic corps, and the Hanok committee in the Seongbuk-gu Office.

Doojin HWANG

Director, Doojin Hwang Architects
#19, Hyojaro-7-gil, Jongno-gu
Seoul, Korea 110-040
www.djharch.com

Architect Doojin Hwang was born in Seoul in 1963. He studied architecture at Seoul National University and Yale University.

Hwang belongs to a select group of architects in Korea who are expert in handling contemporary and traditional projects with professional mastery and cultural sensitivity. In 2010, for example, the Museum of Far Eastern Antiquities in Stockholm, Sweden, selected him as architect for the new Korean Gallery in the historic Tyghuset on Skeppsholmen islet in central Stockholm.

His interest in geometry is a common thread running through his works. He is concerned with manipulating and layering various geometrical orders in space, structure and form. Even his *hanok* works are an exploration of the orthogonal grid system, intrinsic to post-and-lintel wood structure. Alongside an interest in understanding life culture through an historical viewpoint, notably that of Asian modernism, Hwang's architecture aims to go beyond simple formalism.

Hwang is also one of the most sought-after architectural writers in Korea. *Where Is Your Seoul?*, a collection of essays on Seoul, and *Hanok Is Back*, a *hanok*-based architectural treatise, have earned him a reputation in both the theory and practice of architecture.

Hwang has won a number of architectural awards, including the UNESCO Asia-Pacific Cultural Heritage Award, the Acheon Prize from the Korean Institute of Architects and the Prime Minister's Prize at the Korean Architecture Awards. In 2007, he participated in the Megacity Network Contemporary Korean Architecture traveling exhibition in four European cities as both an exhibitor and exhibition designer. In 2010, he represented Korea in the "Active Sustainable Design Now" conference held at the Shanghai Expo. In 2009 and 2014, he gave two lecture tours at several universities and cultural institutions in the US, including the Harvard Graduate School of Design and the Smithsonian. In 2009, he became the first architect to speak at the TEDxSeoul conference.

When he is not working on architecture, Hwang enjoys studying 3D tessellation, which he calls "the 3D version of Escher's drawings." He also likes walking around the Seoul Fortress.

JIWUHEON SPECIALISTS

Master builder Taedo Chung, window specialist Yongshik Shim, roof specialist Jaepil Chae and masonry specialist Sangkyu Park have been involved in many royal palaces, national treasures and private homes throughout Korea, such as Gyeongbokgung Palace and Changdeokgung Palace and many Buddhist temples.

Youngsu JUNG

Hongchungun Suhsukmyeon
Soohari 118-1
Gangwondo, Korea
Tel: 82-2-762-8361
Culture Heritage Carpentry Technician
#1778

Born in 1960, culture heritage carpenter technician Youngsu Jung began his professional career as a carpenter at the age of twenty-two. He traveled and worked around Korea for twenty-seven years restoring national *hanok* and temples. He believes that like the fate between two people there can also be fate between wood and builder. A great *hanok* can only be built with good wood and good carpenters. His earlier projects were primarily renovations of palaces, national treasures and temples, but he is presently undertaking projects for new *hanok* construction in Seoul.

His work includes completion or renovations of the following structures: Eun Deok Cultural Center, Hanwha Training Institute, Kyongbukgung Palace, Namsangol Hanok Village, Korean Cultural Center in California, Jaeneung Educational Institute *hanok*, and residential *hanok* in Bukchon Hanok Village and in the Pyungcahang-dong district of Seoul, as well as elsewhere in Korea.

Bongryol KIM

President, Korea National University of Arts (K-Arts)
35-32, Tongui-dong, Jongno-gu, Seoul
110-040, Korea
Tel: 82-070-4816-6613

Bongryol Kim was born in 1958. He attained his BS, MA and PhD from the Department of Architecture at Seoul National University. He has published numerous books on Buddhist temples and Korean traditional architecture and design, including *Korean Architecture: Traditional Architecture* (1985), *Beobjusa Temple* (1993), *The Architecture of Monastic Vows* (1998) and *The Secret Spirit of Korean Architecture* (2005). Not only is Kim internationally recognized for his publications but he is also known for designing the presidential guest house, "Samcheongjang," the Korean Garden in Frankfurt and the Korea National University of Arts campus in Seoul.

Kim is a committee member of the Ministry of Cultural Heritage, a Director at Arumjigi Culture Keepers Foundation and the President of the Korean Association of Architectural History. He is also currently the President of Korea National University of Arts (K-Arts).

Paiksun KIM
Paik Sun Design Studio
4fl, 8-13, Nonhyeon 1-dong, Gangnam-gu, Seoul, Korea
Tel: 82-2-548-6788
www.paiksundesign.com

Designer/Architect Paiksun Kim, born in 1966, received his BA in oriental painting from Hongik University College of Fine Arts. He is currently CEO at Paik Sun Design Studio and Adjunct Professor in interior architecture at Kyungwon University. Design, architecture, art directing, painting and photography are among his many talents. Through his wide-ranging work, he examines communication between past and present Korean cultures and weaves traditional elements with modern sensibilities. He was won numerous awards for his art, architecture and design.

Moonho LEE
Gaeun & Partners
176, Seongbuk-ro, Seongbuk-gu, Seoul, Korea
Tel: 82-210-8257-7359
in-hanok@hanmail.net

Born in Korea in 1967, Moonho Lee did his undergraduate and graduate studies at the Department of Architectural Engineering, Jung Ang University. In the early years of his career he participated in the development of the Seongbuk-dong Hanok Village project and the construction of the Korea Furniture Museum. In 2006, he established Gaeun & Partners and is currently building *hanok* for private residences and offices in Seoul.

In 2009, Lee received the UNESCO Asia-Pacific Heritage Award for Culture Heritage Conservation and in 2013 the Grand Prix from the Korean Ministry of Land, Infrastructure and Transportation for the Jaeneung Educational Institute, Yulsuwon, Sanchung.

Seungmo SEO
Representative
Samuso Hyojadong, Architects & Associates
1F #39-6 Chongundong, Jongnogu, Seoul, Korea 110-030
Tel: 82-2-720-9052; Fax: 82-2-720-6059
www.samusohyojadong.com
Adjunct Professor, University of Seoul

Seungmo Seo was born in Kyoto, Japan, in 1971. He attained his BA and MA from the Department of Architecture at Kyungwon University in Korea. He then completed his MFA at the Department of Architecture at Tokyo National University of Fine Arts and Music. He began his career as a part-time lecturer at Tokyo National University of Fine Arts and Music in

2002. In 2004, he established RDAUNIT, an architecture office. Shortly after, he established Samuso Hyojadong, Architects & Associates. He is a much sought after speaker and writer on architecture, landscape and design in Korea.

Teo YANG
Teo Yang Studio
Jongrogu Gae-dong 67-22
Seoul, Korea 110-800
Tel: 82-2-3673-2302
www.teoyangstudio.com

Interior designer Teo Yang began his career by traveling widely and working in such vibrant cities as Amsterdam, Berlin and Los Angeles, where he designed luxury interiors for boutique hotels and homes, before moving back to Seoul. He set up Teo Yang Studio in 2009. Over the course of his career, Yang has worked on interior design projects all over South Korea and in Shanghai, some of which have been featured in *Vogue Living*, *Elle Decor* and *Lemon Tree magazine*, among others. He has worked with such legendary designers as Marcel Wanders in Amsterdam. Yang holds degrees from the Art Institute of Chicago and the Art Center College of Design in Pasadena where he studied environmental design. He has published two books on interior design, both of which have been translated and published in China.

Teo Yang Studio specializes in high-end residential and branding commercial projects with an emphasis on modern architecture and custom detailing. The firm brings a fresh approach to elegant, tailored interiors, mixing modern with vintage and high art with personal treasures to create moments of unexpected beauty. "Story-telling" and personal experience through space are priorities in the designs coming out of Teo Yang Studio.

Published by Tuttle Publishing, an imprint of Periplus Editions (HK) Ltd

www.tuttlepublishing.com

ISBN: 978-0-8048-4467-3 (HC)
ISBN: 978-0-8048-5745-1 (PB)

Previously Published in Hardcover as *Hanok: The Korean House*
Library of Congress Control Number 2016469267

Distributed by
North America, Latin America & Europe
Tuttle Publishing
364 Innovation Drive
North Clarendon, VT 05759-9436 U.S.A.
Tel: 1 (802) 773-8930; Fax: 1 (802) 773-6993
info@tuttlepublishing.com; www.tuttlepublishing.com

Japan
Tuttle Publishing
Yaekari Building, 3rd Floor
5-4-12 Osaki, Shinagawa-ku
Tokyo 141-0032
Tel: (81) 3 5437-0171; Fax: (81) 3 5437-0755
sales@tuttle.co.jp; www.tuttle.co.jp

Asia Pacific
Berkeley Books Pte. Ltd.
3 Kallang Sector, #04-01,
Singapore 349278
Tel: (65) 67412178; Fax: (65) 67412179
inquiries@periplus.com.sg; www.tuttlepublishing.com

HC 17 16 15 14   5 4 3 2 1
PB 26 25 24 23   5 4 3 2 1

Printed in China   2309EP

"Books to Span the East and West"

Tuttle Publishing was founded in 1832 in the small New England town of Rutland, Vermont (USA). Our core values remain as strong today as they were then—to publish best-in-class books which bring people together one page at a time. In 1948, we established a publishing outpost in Japan—and Tuttle is now a leader in publishing English-language books about the arts, languages and cultures of Asia. The world has become a much smaller place today and Asia's economic and cultural influence has grown. Yet the need for meaningful dialogue and information about this diverse region has never been greater. Over the past seven decades, Tuttle has published thousands of books on subjects ranging from martial arts and paper crafts to language learning and literature—and our talented authors, illustrators, designers and photographers have won many prestigious awards. We welcome you to explore the wealth of information available on Asia at **www.tuttlepublishing.com**.

Nani Park was born in Korea but grew up in Hawaii, which gives her a special perspective as both an insider and outsider in Korea. Currently residing in Seoul, she lived in a *hanok* when she was young and wanted to share her experience of contemporary *hanok* living. An award-winning illustrator and art educator with a Master's degree in fine arts from the School of Visual Arts in New York, she has worked in the art industry for over two decades.

Robert J. Fouser was born and raised in Ann Arbor, Michigan. He holds a BA in Japanese language and literature and an MA in applied linguistics, both from the University of Michigan, and a PhD in applied linguistics from Trinity College, Dublin. Since 2008 he has taught Korean at Seoul National University. He renovated his own *hanok* in 2012 and has been active in promoting *hanok* preservation.

Jongkeun Lee is one of Korea's leading photographers of interiors, food and products. He established his own studio, Apo Associates (www.apo.co.kr), in 1995 and works actively in the field of advertising. He contributes regularly to design and lifestyle magazines and his photographs are featured in the book *Korea Style*, published by Tuttle Publishing.

TUTTLE

www.tuttlepublishing.com

Printed in China 2309EP

Amidst the glass-and-steel skyscrapers and luxury apartments of modern-day Seoul, traditional Korean houses known as *hanok* survive and play a surprisingly important role. *Inside the Korean House* showcases 12 very special *hanok* that have been selected to reflect the lifestyle of style-conscious Koreans today, in a country where traditional values are still highly respected.

While the exteriors of these homes are indistinguishable from the traditional *hanok* of past decades, the interiors have been adapted to keep up with the times. Traditional stone, wood and clay are still the basic materials used, and the houses make full use of natural elements such as wind and sunlight based on the principles of *baesanimsu*—which position the *hanok* in harmony with the forces of nature and the geography of their sites.

Each *hanok* in this book has a unique story told from the point of view of the owners, many of whom are well-known architects and designers. This book provides an unparalleled look at the lifestyle of contemporary Koreans who are leading the world today in terms of design, fashion and innovation.

ISBN 978-0-8048-5745-1

51999

9 780804 857451   US $19.99